NAMED LOCOMOTIVES
OF BRITISH RAIL

DIESEL AND ELECTRIC

compiled and edited by

MICHAEL OAKLEY

D.BRADFORD BARTON LTD

The prototype electric locomotive for the Manchester to Sheffield line was L.N.E.R. No.6701, built at Doncaster in 1940-1 but then marooned with nowhere to run because of further work being postponed during the Second World War. Until this could be restarted the opportunity was taken to gain service experience with the locomotive by loaning it to the Dutch railways which used the same system of 1,500V d.c. overhead. During its five-year loan period the locomotive acquired the nickname 'Tommy' from its drivers, and on its return to B.R. to become No.26000 the name was made official. The locomotive was thus the first non-steam type of any kind to receive a name on B.R.

Brian Webb

ISBN 0 85153 386 8

Published jointly by **D. BRADFORD BARTON LTD** · **Trethellan House** · **Truro** · **Cornwall**
and the **DIESEL & ELECTRIC GROUP** · 133 Boldmere Road · Sutton Coldfield
Printed by Lovell Baines Print Ltd Newbury Berkshire

WHAT'S IN A NAME?

It is not known who was first inspired to call
a machine a name, but as far as is known the
practice dates almost from the beginnings of
machinery itself - possibly as part of the
love-hate relationship between men and their
mechanical inventions which finds its expression
in names of different kinds. The first railway
locomotives were known by names and this was a
pleasant enough situation when they were few in
number but great in variety, and each had more
claim to being considered an individual entity.
Stephenson's 'Rocket' was, by the standards of
the day, a prime example of the locomotive name
with impact which at the same time encapsulated
the perceived character of its bearer.

The problem was that subsequent mass production
of locomotives soon outpaced the dictionary, and a
host of other appropriate and inappropriate
appellations was seized upon. Locomotives were
named after selected people, causing offence at
times to those who had not been selected; after
places, causing confusion among inexperienced
travellers as to trains' destinations; and
eventually after all manner of things with no
immediate relevance at all, and with every effect
from memorable to laughable.

The nationalised railways in 1948 inherited
stock enough of named steam locomotives and
perhaps wisely confined their elaborations on the
theme to a minimum among the standard steam
locomotives which were built. The result was a
happy balance, and both 'Britannia' at the
beginning of the series and 'Evening Star' at the
end benefitted from not having overmuch competition.
So it was with something close to a clean sheet that
the first construction of main line diesel and
electric locomotives began in quantity, mostly
around a decade after the 'Britannias'. Names
followed spasmodically, and there were soon enough
in service to judge whether the advance in motive
power had inspired a similar advance in standards of
locomotive nomenclature.

The results were mixed. Names of the largest
mountains in the country applied to the heaviest
locomotives in the country had an appealing
congruence, as well as being memorable for being
few in number, and far more locomotives came to be
known as 'Peaks' than ever carried Peak names. By
contrast the names of ocean liners applied to
locomotives which worked the Euston to Liverpool
boat trains were less inventive, at a time when the
ocean liner traffic was about to be decimated by
air passenger transport. The later application to
'Peaks' of regimental names perpetuated a railway
tradition and shared with the ocean liner names a
delight in visual detail: the flags of the
steamship lines were picked out within an integral
nameplate casting on the latter, while the
military designations were adorned by castings of
regimental crests. Perhaps the most effective
names, however, were those which modestly adorned
some of the electric locomotives on the Manchester
to Sheffield line, with their evocation of ancient
history and mythology from a time when the
foundations of modern science were first beginning
to be laid. Mythology implies a belief in the
existence of better things, while history implies
the development of knowledge to attain them. On
this combination of looking both to the past and
the future, names were first applied to modern
locomotives on British Railways.

The Woodhead was primarily a heavy freight route, and few of its locomotives received boilers for heating passenger trains. Those which did came at the end of the number series and also received names from ancient history and mythology formerly borne by Great Central Railway steam locomotives which had worked over the route. Nevertheless the passenger batch also worked on freight, which is what would have brought No.26051 'Mentor' to Wath depot, where it is seen resting on a Sunday in 1960. The nameplates were removed after the Woodhead line lost its passenger services in 1970, certain locomotives being renumbered in a different order so as to group together different sorts of braking system and other features. In 1980 the line was threatened with imminent closure due to changing traffic patterns, which will mean scrap for the locomotives as no other line now uses the same system.

                                                                                          Brian Webb

The larger version of the Woodhead design is Class EM2, later B.R. Class 77. These seven locomotives were all nominally for passenger traffic, being geared for a theoretical 90m.p.h. maximum in spite of their own line having a limit of 65. The name 'Pandora' was fitted at Gorton Works in 1959 to No.27006, seen here outside Manchester (Piccadilly) in its final B.R: livery of green with small yellow warning end. Passenger traffic over the Woodhead route latterly consisted of five-coach trains only in most cases, for which the smaller Class 76 locomotives had ample power, so the larger type was made redundant without receiving its allocated renumbering as Class 77. The locomotives were sold to the Dutch railways where they remain in service, ironically with nameplates removed.

Brian Webb Collection

Although higher-powered diesels were drafted to the Anglo-Scottish expresses before electrification was completed in 1974, Class 40s could be found to the end on less important workings. This working is the summer relief Birmingham to Edinburgh train, seen at Crewe on 22 July 1970. For all their low power, the Class 40s have an excellent reputation for reliability, and this example is running in conspicuously clean condition from having been on Royal Train duty. No.233 is, appropriately, 'Empress of England'.

Derek Cross

The original 'Peaks' were named after well-known mountains, starting with the highest in England, Scafell Pike, and working downwards with some omissions. At first the ten locomotives were used both on the West Coast main line from Euston and on the Midland line from St.Pancras, and for a while were the most powerful locomotives owned by B.R. Development was rapid, however, No.D2 'Helvellyn' being used in uprated condition as a prototype for the improved engine fitted to later construction. The original 'Peaks' were then banished to freight work at Toton depot, for which their gear ratio fitted them better than passenger work. This view is of the early 'Peak' heyday in September 1960, with No.D4 'Great Gable' passing Luton with a down express.

John C. Baker

The second construction series of B.R./Sulzer Type 4s is also universally known as the 'Peaks', though the only names applied to some of them at random were of local regiments on the Midland line. With their high power output at both ends of the speed range, the 2,500b.h.p. version of the design has now nearly monopolised the express service from St.Pancras for two decades, successfully resisting attempted invasions by the more powerful but less suitably geared Brush/Sulzer version of the same design. An unbalanced working has produced two named 'Peaks' on this Derby to London train, which will almost certainly be travelling at 90m.p.h. or more as it passes Glendon North Junction, at the foot of one of many banks on this line, on 12 April 1975. The train engine is No.45.143 '5th Royal Inniskilling Dragoon Guards', newly renumbered into the TOPS series of computer-style numbers after conversion to electric train heating. The pilot locomotive is No.D53 'Royal Tank Regiment', still with its old number and steam train heating. In spite of having no equipment for working in multiple, which was removed early in their life due to lack of use, 'Peaks' were quite often used to double-head Derby trains for the purpose of moving spare locomotives around the country, and two drivers would be required on this run.

F.R.Kerr

Generally the named Class 45s were kept among those chosen partly at.random for conversion to electric train heating in the 1970s, and they have remained on the St.Pancras expresses. On this duty at Sheffield on 8 June 1977 is former No.D61, now 45.112 'The Royal Army Ordnance Corps'. On the right is Class 46 No.46.047 on a Lickey route express. Replacement of headcode boxes with marker lights has left little outward difference between the two classes, but the Class 45/1 is given away by the E.T.H. jumper cable looped round the nearest buffer, while the Class 46 still has a steam pipe to the right of the coupling.

Alan Brooke Baylis

Detail of No.45.137 'The Bedfordshire and Hertfordshire Regiment (T.A.)' at St.Pancras on 13 September 1978.

Ray King

OLD UNCLE TOM COBBLEIGH AND HALL. . . .

   With the multi-regional steam 'Britannias', B.R.
had sought to achieve a multi-regional naming
policy - though of course individual names remained
strongly one-regional in themselves. Scottish
examples, named after Scottish firths, found this
no impediment, unlike the ones distinguished with
names from former locomotives of their ungrateful
recipients in the West. Only at Cardiff, always an
area apart within the Great Western, was anything
much made of them, and they were soon transferred
away, while 'Evening Star' itself was confined to
breaking records on the non-G.W.R. Somerset & Dorset
line.

   For the problem with the Great Western, as it
still tended to think itself, was not only that it
thought it knew better than anyone else, but also
that a lot of the time it was right. The resultant
combination of insularity and solidarity served it
amply well for many years as far as locomotive
construction was concerned, but with locomotive
names standardisation on desirable property for
inspiration was carried to excess. In the first of
the many policy turnabouts which characterised the
early years of B.R., the attempt to standardise the
Western with the 'Britannias' was followed by a
period of fluidity in which the Region essentially
resumed designing and naming locomotives of its own.

   In spite of having pioneered the diesel railcar
in the 1930s, the Western took its first step
towards main line modern traction with the
experimental gas turbine locomotives 18000 and
18100 in the 1950s. Tradition dies hard, however,
and one sensed a lack of enthusiasm for the
project in the lack of official names for the
locomotives - the unofficial name 'Kerosene Castle'
being bestowed upon 18000 with something less than
affection. When the diesels did come in main line
locomotive form, they were the peculiarly Western
diesel-hydraulics, with German design engines but
a Western enough high speed performance
characteristic. A decidedly Western outlook on
names saw all the first three types lumped
together as the 'Warship' Classes. Some ill-
defined association between the railway and the
Royal Navy at Plymouth was seized upon as
justification for vessel names applied throughout
the class, not quite in 'Castle' Class numbers but
with nameplates in the same bold serif-style
letterface, with 'Warship Class' suffix. Some

confusion was caused by changes to the
construction programme as it progressed, with some
later names being changed before they were applied.
One name was never applied at all, the locomotive
instead commemorating the centenary of the Royal
Naval Reserve, while incongruously at the head of
the second 'Warship' series went the name of the
retiring chairman of the British Transport
Commission, who can have had little or nothing to
do with the construction of the locomotive which
honoured him.

   More turnabouts in policy were impending, but
not before the Western had completed its last and
most independent fling. The first example of its
final diesel-hydraulic class emerged in a defiant
new bodyshell design, a defiant new range of
independent liveries, and with a new design of
co-ordinated number/nameplates defiantly lettered
'Western Enterprise'. So indeed it was, in all
these respects and more, unquestionably the single
most apposite name ever carried by a B.R.
locomotive. Once again it was only too
unfortunate that so many examples were built, for
the Western names soon exceeded their potential
Too many were merely rehashed 'Warship' names
like 'Western Monarch', while others became
cliches as when unusual destinations were reached
by 'Western Invader'. At least the series
revived near the end with 'Western Renown' and
'Western Glory'.

   After that the attempt to Westernise a few of
the rival diesel-electrics was probably doomed to
indifference anyway, and did not help itself by
abandoning the G.W.R.-style letterface in mid-
series. The appearance on the worst runner of
the batch of the hallowed name 'City of Truro'
was perhaps the last straw, for with this series
the Western-style namings came to a halt.

The first of the diesel-hydraulics was No.D600 'Active'. Due to pressure on B.R. workshops capacity this was one of many orders successfully tendered for by private manufacturers. In this case the diamond-shaped works plate beneath the running number displays the name of the North British Locomotive Company, who had tried to break out of the steam age by arranging to manufacture German M.A.N. diesel engines under licence. Unfortunately this did not stop them from eventually going bankrupt, and their diesel products were criticised for steam-standard workmanship, as well as in this Class the excessive weight of the body design (derived from that of L.M.S. diesel-electric No.10000), plus poor adhesion of the A1A-A1A wheel arrangement with two axles unpowered. There was still time for optimism when this photograph was taken, however, with the locomotive newly arrived on Western Region from Glasgow and bearing the first nameplate to be given to a B.R. 'pilot scheme' diesel.   Brian Webb Collection

Much lighter than the original North British design was the Swindon-built 'Warship', this time using Maybach engines and getting 2,000 or 2,200 nominal b.h.p. (the actual setting was 2,304 in most cases) into a B-B configuration. One example was tried with Paxman engines at 2,400b.h.p., and this was No.D830 'Majestic', seen here at Bristol in January 1968. The front end design is also German, at any rate in inspiration, being a scaled-down version of the similar V200 design used beneath the more generous loading gauge of the Deutsche Bundesbahn. On the left is the very different front end of a 'Western'.

P.J.Fowler

An independent design consultant was used for the last hydraulic design and continued the strong tradition of distinctive bodyline but in a very different style from the 'Warships'. The extra length of the C-C design was terminated in a flat front to markedly impressive effect, while other features of the design were also used for innovations. A noticeable sign of the new broom was the abandonment of serif-style letterface on the nameplates, which instead were produced to a new style with numberplates to match. The letters were in silver finish generally on a black background and needed little maintenance to keep them clean. In spite of the poor condition of the paintwork all around, the low evening light picks out the numberplate of No.D1073 'Western Bulwark' clearly as it backs onto the 13.05 Penzance to Liverpool train at Bristol on 14 August 1967.

P.J.Fowler

Side view of a 'Western', showing the nameplate centrally placed on the symmetrical bodyside, but with the numberplate at the driver's corner only balanced in the early livery arrangement by the round badge at the other end of the type normally used on coaching stock. No.D1012 'Western Firebrand' is heading west from Bristol with parcels stock on a day in 1968.
                                                                                                P.J.Fowler

The basic soundness of the 'Western' as a visual entity was reflected in the minimal change which occurred when repainted in later B.R. blue livery. The full yellow front end actually co-ordinated better with the existing lines of the body than had the previous small panel, while the B.R. double arrow went conveniently in the same place as the badge it replaced. The 'Westerns' were thus notable for the consistency with which these features of the new livery were applied, in contrast to the many positions found for the double arrow on the 'Warships'. One unsightly feature for a time was the painting-out of the 'D' prefix to the number when such prefixes were generally abolished on B.R., and it is in this condition that No.D1001 'Western Pathfinder' is seen passing Aller Junction with an up express in July 1976.
                                                                                                T.A.Shutler

The last series of names applied by Western Region before the period of restraint were those to the
Class 47s, which were then joining the hydraulics on principal duties. Names were chosen which had been
borne by previous Western locomotives, 'North Star' having been a famous broad gauge engine built by
Stephensons in Newcastle to haul the first public train on the Great Western Railway. Today's 'North
Star' is seen in the form of No.47.077 on less spectacular duty, negotiating the sharp curve at
St.Andrew's Junction with a Paddington to Birmingham express on 9 October 1975. The nameplate is in
similar style to those of the 'Westerns', but with bolder letterface and obviously less solid border.

Philip D. Hawkins

Later examples of this batch had nameplates which reverted to the traditional bolder letterface with large block serifs, as used on G.W.R. steam locomotive nameplates. Nearly all of the locomotives which carried the ex-G.W.R. names were kept on Western Region allocation, though one of their many appearances elsewhere became permanent when Stratford shed was unaccountably allowed to take possession of No.47.085 'Mammoth'. To emphasise its new allegiance the locomotive also acquired the Stratford trademark of a silver roof, later changed to cream - allegedly the result of Stratford becoming fed up of losing its own locomotives, though it also reflected a concern for appearances sadly not equalled elsewhere. In this condition the locomotive is seen restarting from Colchester with the 09.30 Liverpool Street to Norwich express, the light colour of the roof standing out through the murk of an April day in 1979.
M.J.Collins

The nameplate of No.47.085, undergoing attention at Crewe Works on 5 May 1979.
Malcolm Clements

ENTERPRISE AND RESTRAINT

The basis largely of individual lines or regions on which namings of modern B.R. locomotives developed was paralleled by a similar line of development in the private sector. Perceiving the slow progress B.R. were making towards meeting the obvious large demand for new diesels, several manufacturers built their own prototypes. Semi-prototype locomotives there had been on B.R. before, from the L.M.S. No.10000 of 1947 onwards, though all these were built or purchased by the railway and none ever developed into a production run or carried a name. This time the prototypes remained the property of the manufacturers and were offered to B.R. for trials in the hope that substantial production orders would follow.

First and pre-eminent among the prototypes was the English Electric 'Deltic', put on rails in 1954. This featured twin high speed triangular opposèd-piston engines of a type uséd in naval gunboats and offered high performance in exchange for high maintenance cost. English Electric found no name for the subsequent prototype diesel DP2, but a rival Birmingham/Sulzer machine gloried in the name 'Lion'. The trio was completed by the Brush/Maybach 'Falcon'. With the advantage of singularity, as well as of instantly-recognisable liveries, all these locomotives became well-known by their names alone, which succeeded mainly through their very simplicity in evoking all the acknowledged attributes of the creatures referred to. Brush continued the bird theme into a series with 'Hawk' and 'Kestrel', while a further named prototype on B.R. came from the Yorkshire Engine Company in the form of the unsuccessful diesel shunter 'Taurus'.

Perhaps inspired by the enterprise of the manufacturers, B.R. at length bestowed names upon the production series 'Deltics', which followed the prototype onto top link express passenger services on the East Coast main line. As usual tradition was a powerful influence, and the North Eastern as well as Scottish allocations received the names of local army regiments, in most cases with cast regimental crest surmounting the nameplates in G.W.R.-style bold serif lettering. For once some publicity value was extracted, the locomotives being worked to appropriate places such as Dumfries and Inverness on troop trains for special ceremonies. The Finsbury Park allocation saw no ceremony but followed a different tradition, receiving the names of famous racehorses. The advantage of being few in number once again contributed to perhaps the most deservedly memorable series of all.

Unhappily any further inspiration in this direction was stifled just as a successful formula had appeared, as a result of the accession to high places in B.R. of executives who apparently declared names to be an unnecessary extravagance. Just when the worst ramifications of the naming policy of Western Region had reached a hiatus, the more careful and effective choices being made elsewhere were also brought to a halt. This situation was to last over a decade, during which most locomotives retained their existing names but quite a few were allowed to lose them. In 1970 the electrics of the Woodhead route lost first their passenger workings and then the nameplates of the 'passenger' examples; some were withdrawn altogether, while all of Class EM2 were sold to the country which had named the first EM1, ironically losing their names in the process. The Class 40s, as they were now designated, mostly had their ocean liner names removed and placed into store or sold, and many of the earlier Western Region names disappeared as first the 'Warships' and then the 'Westerns' themselves were withdrawn. The named Class 47s, with two exceptions, were not at first among the examples chosen for conversion to electric train heating when that was standardised, and no particular attention seems to have been given to looking after their nameplates while on freight work.

A further casualty of the latest policy turnaround was that several Class 37s in East Anglia got as far as being seen with new nameplates boarded over awaiting ceremonial unveiling, only to have them quietly removed again when the army regiments which provided the names inconveniently ceased to exist.

The most powerful diesel locomotive in the world, it was called, and with every justification, for at the time of its construction the 3,300b.h.p. of the prototype 'Deltic' gave it nearly double the installed power of its nearest rival on B.R. and nearly three times the power-weight ratio. The imposing bodyshell was finished in a startling livery of powder blue with cream stripes, the name 'Deltic' (derived from the triangular shape of the opposed-piston engines in an inverted Greek letter Delta) being painted on the bodyside centrally between the stripes. The locomotive spent most of its trial running on the West Coast main line and adjuncts, where it was - incredibly - rejected by the engineers of the day on grounds of capital cost. The East Coast main line had no such qualms and ordered a number to take over all the fastest workings on the route. The prototype spent its last days before being retired for preservation making E.C.M.L. trips for crew familiarisation, and is seen here in full cry, and doubtless well ahead of schedule, passing Sandy with an up express in August 1960.

John C. Baker

The likeliest contender, it was at first thought, in the Type 4 prototype stakes was the product of the consortium which included Associated Electrical Industries and its builders, the Birmingham Railway Carriage & Wagon Company of Smethwick. Sulzer Brothers contributed the engine, which was the latest version of that installed in the earlier 'Peaks'. The locomotive ran the customary gamut of trials, high speed performances being recorded on the East Coast main line and on its 'home' line of Wolverhampton to Paddington. However, much trouble was apparently experienced with the electrical systems, and before this could be resolved B.R.C.W. was overtaken by bankruptcy, allegedly in consequence of its work on Southern Region Class 33s. The locomotive was consigned to a siding at Smethwick for a long time and eventually was broken up for scrap to pay off creditors. To some extent its construction was futile, since B.R. did not wait to evaluate it before standardising on the same Sulzer engine for their new Class 47 design to be built mainly by Brush, but at least it survives in part, for its engine was eventually re-used in a Class 47. Here it is seen in happier days, during the technical testing phase of its brief career. With its livery even more startling than that of the prototype 'Deltic', the white body and gold stripes standing out against the foliage, it is awaiting restart with a test train on the 1 in 37.7 Lickey Incline just north of Bromsgrove station in August 1962.

A.E.I./Brian Webb Collection

The named rival to 'Lion' was the Brush locomotive 'Falcon', which took its name from the Falcon Works at Loughborough. In spite of having the now-standard electric transmission, the locomotive allied it with twin Maybach engines of the same type as used in the 'Westerns', but set to a still higher output of 2,880b.h.p. This apparently impressed B.R. less than the reliability of the Brush electrical equipment, and the eventual B.R. standard Class 47 order was given mostly to Brush using the 'Falcon' electrics with a 'Lion' bodyshell and engine, though numerous detail changes were made. 'Falcon' itself, however, led a surprisingly long and productive life, at first on the East Coast main line and later on Western Region alongside its Maybach cousins. It was eventually taken into B.R. stock, losing the prototype number D0280 in favour of the designation 1200, though it did not survive to become Class 53 as provided in the TOPS scheme. 'Falcon's' demise came due to unsuitability for conversion to electric train heating, and although it stayed in service for a while on freight duty from Newport, it was eventually sold for scrap. A condition of the sale was immediate destruction, in spite of a bid to save it for preservation. Back at the beginning of its career, 'Falcon' poses at Loughborough, showing the cast motif on the bodyside and the two-tone green livery (originally with light predominating, but later reversed).

Brush

1B20
D0280
THE MASTER CUTLER
1Z00
D 0280
FALCON

An early prototype diesel was the 'hood' type unit No.10800 of 1950, built by the North British Locomotive Company and fitted with an 827b.h.p. Paxman engine. The subsequent B.R. 'Pilot Scheme' order for ten locomotives of 800b.h.p. also went to North British for a similar design (the No.D8400 series of 1958), but after that the prototype locomotive was more-or-less unwanted. It was acquired by Brush Traction for use on research work into squirrel cage traction motors and generators without commutators. In this photograph it is seen in 'Falcon' works during November 1962, being fitted with the spare Maybach engine originally acquired for the 'Falcon' locomotive, with which it ran at a setting of 140b.h.p. Continuing the theme of birds of prey, Brush gave it the name 'Hawk', though this was never carried and the locomotive retained its existing number below which was painted the legend 'Research Locomotive' in small capitals. Low-speed test trips were run on the former Great Central line between Leicester and Nottingham, with some success but not enough to warrant continuing with the project. In 1972 the engine was removed for use with a standby generator for 'Falcon' Works, and the locomotive was cut up in 1976.

Brush

Some of the work done on 'Hawk' was incorporated in the next and last Brush prototype, but mainly it was
the change to alternating current generators (alternators) for main line traction which formed the most
revolutionary feature of 'Kestrel'. This diesel-electric Co-Co design was intended to show B.R. the way
for the future, being fitted with the latest Sulzer engine of allegedly 4,000b.h.p., whence the parent
company Hawker Siddeley gave it the number HS4000. The locomotive was completed in 1967 and turned out
in another startling livery, this time orange and chocolate with the name painted centrally along the
bodyside. Hopes crumbled almost immediately when the locomotive was found to be chronically overweight
at 133 tons, as well as producing below-par power output. It spent most of its time on slow speed heavy
freight work, having been found no better than a 'Deltic' on the East Coast main line before it was
banned from express running because of its weight. This view is of its only other passenger working, on
the traditional demonstration from Marylebone to Princes Risborough in January 1968. In 1971 it was
abruptly sold to Russia, whence little has been heard of it since. Perhaps the main achievement of
'Kestrel' was to nail once and for all the coffin of the mixed-traffic locomotive in favour of a
reversion to specialisation in the later B.R. heavy freight Class 56.   Brush

One further prototype completed the range of named examples to run on B.R., though like the Brush 'Hawk' it never actually carried the allotted name. This was the 'Taurus' diesel-mechanical shunter of the Yorkshire Engine Company, which had a brief trial in the early 1960s. Its mechanical inspiration was yet another prototype, the B.R.-Fell locomotive No.10100 of some years before, which featured an extraordinary arrangement of four small engines driving a massive mechanical transmission on a 2-D-2 wheel arrangement. 'Taurus' was a more modest conception, applying the Fell principle of gear change without loss of tractive effort to a high-powered shunting locomotive. This time twin engines were tried, on a 0-8-0 wheel arrangement, the locomotive being in other respects derived from its makers' successful designs used in industry - the twin-engine 0-6-0 diesel-electric 'Janus' (also given an even briefer trial on B.R.) and 0-8-0 diesel-hydraulic 'Indus' classes. Yorkshire's other design for B.R., the diminutive Class 02 dock shunter, had a successful career for some years, featuring the customary Yorkshire use of Rolls Royce engines. Not so the 'Taurus' design, where the 600b.h.p. installed power was not enough to overcome insoluble problems with the mechanical transmission. The example tried on B.R. (Yorkshire Works No.2875) was taken back by its makers and eventually cut up for scrap shortly before the business closed down. Here it is seen out of action on B.R. at Swindon on 13 May 1961. The only other example constructed was exported to Spain.

R.C.Riley

It was some time before the production series 'Deltics' were delivered, after a famous series of delays, and some time more before names were bestowed, but there is no mistaking the centre of attention in this view. In the original two-tone green livery plus small yellow warning panel, No.D9018 'Ballymoss' is the racehorse waiting to leave Edinburgh for London with the up 'Heart of Midlothian' express on 16 April 1966.

Derek Cross

The favourite unscheduled use for 'Deltics' has always been at depot open days, where spare ones can always be provided no matter how rare they may be for enthusiast special trains! 'Argyll and Sutherland Highlander' has come over from Haymarket to Eastfield depot open day in Glasgow on 17 September 1972 to be given a pipe welcome. Slightly less welcome, it would appear, are visitors, the 'Deltic' cab being fastened up unlike those of other locomotives alongside. To the left is the first West Coast electric locomotive to run in Scotland albeit not under power as the line was not then electrified, No.83.005.

Derek Cross

Towards the end of the 1970s the 'Deltics' at last relinquished premier place on the East Coast main line to new High Speed Trains, but they continued in use on secondary services. Ample scope for this was provided by the 1979 Penmanshiel Tunnel disaster, in which a rockfall blocked the main line for five months while a new route was constructed around it. Improvised workings at this time included many diversions onto the West Coast main line via Carstairs, over which Edinburgh (Haymarket) drivers learned the road to Carlisle. It is at Carstairs itself that No.55.014 was photographed leaving with an emergency working for Edinburgh, just before the proper route reopened, on 18 August 1979.   D.G.Cameron

Racehorse in the stable: 'Meld' hidden among the locomotives waiting outside Doncaster Works on 30 June 1979. Too often this has been the scene in recent years, as 'Deltics' phased off the fastest workings no longer merited the fastest of Doncaster's attention. This one at least is waiting for repair and not just for cannibalisation and is given away as a 'runner' by the white windscreen surround applied in 1979 to several of the best examples.

A.E.Neal

No.76.049, relegated to freight work at Valehouse near Hadfield, with a train of empties on 24 August 1979. Formerly 'Jason', this locomotive has joined its colleagues in running with nameplates no longer.

Geoff Pinder

IN A SPIRIT OF AMBIGUITY

Whatever the reason for restraint on the part of B.R., the nameplates of diesels soon began to join those of steam locomotives in the hands of collectors. B.R. themselves became involved in this, selling used nameplates direct to the public in their 'Collectors' Corner'.

In spite of all this, or perhaps because of it, yet another turnabout in B.R. policy was impending and the end of the 1970s saw the first results of the avowedly more publicity-conscious approach adopted by the British Railways Board under Sir Peter Parker. The Stephenson Locomotive Society was allowed to bestow the name 'Stephenson' upon one of the latest electric locomotives. Then in 1977 came the opening of the floodgates with the allocation of names to the other 35 Class 87 electrics and the fifty Class 50 diesels. The cost was quoted at £15,592, this being justified as an investment by the B.R. spokesman on the grounds that the plates would sell for far more after use. With inflation this will doubtless be true if the 87s run their projected lifespan of forty years. . .

But whatever else it achieved, the new policy undoubtedly reactivated all the old controversy as to the justification or otherwise both of names in general and these names in particular. On the positive side, a welcome return was made to extracting publicity value from naming ceremonies, such as those for No.50.035, named 'Ark Royal' to coincide with the decommissioning of that vessel, or for electric locomotives named after cities; while many enthusiasts who like names for their own sake could not fail to be pleased. On the debit side, Class 50 suffered a mass rehash of the 'Warship' names, many of them still warm from their previous use, while Class 87 fared still worse with a mix-up of old steam locomotives, real and fictitious Scotsmen, and the names of persons who died before railways were even invented. Worst of all, perhaps, was the adoption of a totally standardised style of nameplate for these and all subsequent cases, except for a few Class 50s which also received a crest. The results, applied to the ugly and disappointing Class 87 and the boxes-of-tricks-on-wheels Class 50, amounted to an opportunity really to give a new character to modern traction thrown away.

A gradual amelioration followed, presumably through subsequent names being chosen less precipitately. Three regions have bestowed names on Class 47s which have overcome the ambiguity of historical associations through the benefit of being severely limited in numbers, thereby proving once again that quality matters more than quantity in locomotive names. Class 86 electrics have similarly benefitted from greater selectivity. Perhaps the most genuinely original name of any ever carried by a B.R. locomotive, however ambiguous its connotations, is now paraded by No.47.555 'The Commonwealth Spirit', and even a non-locomotive has been favoured for the first time since Pullman cars with the naming of a power car for one Advanced Passenger Train after its birthplace, the City of Derby.

And amid all this there is another spirit of enterprise manifesting itself once again. It began with the appearance of home-made nameplates 'Great Eastern' on one of that line's regulars, removed amid recriminations but soon replaced with official plates on another locomotive, while county names were bestowed upon others. Love-hate fundamentals reasserted themselves with names such as 'Dracula' mischievously applied to a Class 40, while unoccupied shunting crews have made several Class 08s their own. This time the names have mostly stayed, which shows that originality can still win through.

The nameplates provided by the Stephenson Locomotive Society for the resumption of locomotive naming are a distinctive burnished metal design with black lettering, and under the name 'Stephenson' the words 'Named by the Stephenson Locomotive Society 1975'. Originally fitted to the first Class 87 for the West Coast main line extension of through electric working to Glasgow, No.87.001, the nameplates were by agreement later transferred to the last, No.87.101, which is the test locomotive built for trials of thyristor control equipment which permits greater output to be maintained during initial acceleration. The advantages of thyristor control are most obvious in heavy freight work, which the Class 87s perform in the form of nighttime Freightliner trains over Shap. During the day, however, they are almost exclusively on express passenger, and it is a train of the latest Mk.III passenger stock which No.87.101 has brought to the buffers at Euston on 28 April 1979.

Antony R. Guppy

The English Electric candidate from the days of 'Lion' and 'Falcon' was the locomotive DP2, though no name was found for it, and for a time the mass construction of Brush/Sulzer Class 47s gave the impression that English Electric had lost out in spite of their latest prototype's conspicuous success. When an order did eventually come, for the present Class 50, the design was complicated by B.R. stipulations and the class spent an unhappy period working between Crewe and Glasgow before electrification. Transfer to Western Region made them even less popular at first, but with the demise of the hydraulics the Class 50s are the most obviously Western diesel of the present time. Thus the choice fell on them to rejuvenate the railway association with the sea at Plymouth, and the decommissioning of H.M.S. Ark Royal was made the occasion to inaugurate the new official naming policy. No.50.035 is the locomotive which now carries the name and ornamental crest, seen here between workings at Birmingham (New Street) on 17 June 1978.

Alan Brooke Baylis

No.50.022 'Anson' leaving Plymouth with the 09.46 to Paddington
on 29 August 1978.
Les Bertram

The standard style of nameplate adopted for the latest wave of namings, with silver letters and outline on a red background, is seen here on West Coast electric No.87.013 'John O'Gaunt'. The exceptionally high-geared Class 87 (its continuous traction rating is quoted at a speed of 87m.p.h.) suffers from a tendency to slip on starting, so it is a slow restart on this occasion, 28 July 1979, for one of the few expresses still to call at Bletchley.
Geoff Pinder

Although it now heads a new list of names with the appellation 'Royal Scot', No.87.001 still carries a reminder of its days as 'Stephenson' in the form of a cabside running number set lower than normal for the class. Here it is passing Leyland at full speed with the 12.45 Euston to Glasgow on 25 September 1978.

Chris Perkins

An odd choice for the distinction, now that the class has few top rank express workings on its former main lines, No.47.500 nevertheless now carries the name 'Great Western' in the standard new style, but supplemented by a plate carrying the G.W.R. coat of arms beneath the nameplate. A curiosity is that the coat of arms is in its proper unadorned square form on one side of the locomotive but carried on a circular surround on the other.

Chris Perkins

Names came to East Anglia at the third attempt, following the failure first of the official ones for Class 37 and then of the unofficial 'Great Eastern' name applied to No.47.460. The latter returned elsewhere when the Norwich line failed to receive its expected 'cascade' of electrically heated stock, so the official 'Great Eastern' plates are now carried by steam-heated No.47.169. The names of the five East Anglian counties have similarly been applied to steam-heated locomotives - though further conversions to electric are now definitely scheduled - incidentally causing local controversy when B.R. correctly followed the incorrect local government usage in some names with both a 'County of' prefix and a '-shire' suffix. No such problem affects No.47.180 'County of Suffolk', here basking with its Stratford cream roof in the sunshine at Norwich in the spring of 1979.   J.A.Howie

The final series of Class 47 names for the time being seems to be for the batch of twelve examples fitted with electronic controls for working push-pull services between Glasgow and Edinburgh. Pending delivery of new push-pull stock, however, the locomotives had been put to use on any duty to which they were suited, both in and out of Scotland. On 11 August 1979 No.47.701 had wandered no further than Carstairs, where it is waiting to return to Edinburgh with the rear portion of the 12.05 from Birmingham. Visible on the front end are the carriage lighting jumper cables through which push-pull control will be effected electronically, while the Stratford-style cream roof is peculiar to certain examples only.

D.G.Cameron

Named locomotives traditionally are associated with passenger traffic, but 'Taurus' the shunter was by no means the only one to spend all its time on freight work. Certain Class 45s which missed the queue for conversion to Class 45/1 with electric train heating have now had their train-heating boilers isolated as well. This loss, however, is the gain of Southern Region, on which for many years the only named locomotives regularly to visit certain areas were those which came down off the Midland line with merry-go-round coal trains. Seen here is the best-known working, from Welbeck in Nottinghamshire to Northfleet cement works, which conveys 2,000-ton loads around South London and for which standard motive power was a 47 and 45 in tandem. The named locomotive on 5 September 1979 is No.45.043 'The King's Own Royal Border Regiment', seen unloading at the Northfleet terminal in partnership with No.47.201. The reason for the unusual pairing on this working is that the Class 45 has the superior adhesion and brake force, but the Class 47 has the slow-speed control needed for automatic unloading. No named locomotive has yet been slow-speed fitted, and Class 50s had their built-in slow-speed equipment removed before nameplates were fitted. Now this scene too has disappeared, the Northfleet working having been taken over in late 1979 by locomotives of the new heavy freight Class 56 working singly with the same load.
M.J.Collins

The unofficial name 'Newmarketeer' which appeared without explanation on No.45.130 in 1978, seen at Chesterfield on 8 October. The nameplates remained in place for some days, apparently defying several attempts to remove them.

C.Jagger

The fate suffered by No.47.079, whose nameplates were replaced after being missing for some time, considerably shortened from their former glory of 'George Jackson. . .'. The locomotive was photographed in modified condition at Gloucester on 6 May 1979.

Graham F.Scott-Lowe

Among the locomotives which retained their nameplates throughout the period of restraint were the original 'Peaks' now designated Class 44 - only for them to be removed just when naming of other classes restarted! Repeated threats to withdraw the surviving examples, however, have made them a focus of enthusiast interest and the names are restored for special occasions. No.44.008 'Penyghent' was restored to its former glory for the occasion of Toton depot open day in June 1979. No other depot now knows the class, and their workings are restricted in consequence, which doubtless accounted for a large turnout to see them. Here the locomotive is giving footplate rides to visitors, resplendent in nameplates and customised livery.

Antony R. Guppy

The retrogressive side of Class 86 naming is seen in the re-use of the titles of old steam locomotives - though the names themselves are not too obviously of ancient origin. One of the better ones is 'Phoenix', now carried by No.86.219, seen here crossing Crawford viaduct with a northbound special on 27 August 1979.

D.G.Cameron

By reputation the most consistent performers in the West Coast fleet of all are the three locomotives of the hybrid Class 86/1 with Class 87 bogies. Revealing its mechanical details at Willesden depot in December 1978 is No.86.101, now named after a distinguished railwayman of the immediate past, 'Sir William A Stanier F R S'. Nameplate fixing on all electric locomotives is carried out at this, their principal depot, taking two men several hours to secure each plate onto the complicated body structure so that it is thief-proof.
Brian Morrison

No class of locomotives, named or otherwise, provoked a ballyhoo to equal that which surrounded the withdrawal of the last few 'Westerns'. 'Western Fusilier' (D1023) was one of the two favourites for the many special railtours which were run - the other being D1013 'Western Ranger' - and both received livery embellishments such as red backgrounds to D1013's nameplates. For a time it was also predicted that D1013 would be the officially preserved example at York, but in the event that distinction fell to D1023 as well. Here it briefly pre-empts its permanent arrival by working a day trip from Kings Cross, seen being greeted by unprecedented crowds on arrival on 20 November 1976. Passing alongside on the centre road is 'Deltic' No.55.006 'The Fife and Forfar Yeomanry' with the down 'Flying Scotsman'.

Graham F. Scott-Lowe

Number detail of 55.006 showing the coat of arms of the city of York, applied to all 'Deltics' transferred to York depot in 1979.

A.E.Neal

The first of the several 'Westerns' now preserved on ex-B.R. branch lines was D1062 'Western Courier' of
the Western Locomotive Association. This locomotive also spent a period out of use on the Swindon
turntable, and so was a convenient choice for restoration in the works to the early style of maroon
livery. Its first location away from B.R. was on the Torbay Steam Railway - though in this case only
inches away as it poses next to the B.R. empty carriage line at Paignton on 31 August 1977.

Chris Perkins

The nameplate specially recast for preserved No.D1062 after the
originals had been disposed of by B.R. It is distinguishable by
being slightly deeper than standard.   A.E.Neal

Another form of preservation, in a sense, though there is little rest for these ex-B.R. locomotives sold into industrial service. The former Class 08s are now in use at the Foster Yeoman Merehead Quarry stone terminal, where they are seen moving a loaded train through the washing plant prior to collection by the B.R. main line locomotive which will come up the branch from Witham. In contrast to the B.R. policy of naming main line locomotives only, both have had names painted onto the toolboxes by their new owners. B.R. No.D3002 is now No.11 'Dulcote' and No.D3003 is now No.22 'Merehead'.   Graham F.Scott-Lowe

The unofficial name applied - and apparently officially tolerated - on the resident Class 08 shunter at Wolverton carriage works, No.08.806, is 'Bradwell', the name of a nearby village where many works staff live, and the annual works open day is known as more of a family event than an attraction for visiting enthusiasts. It was at the open day on 18 August 1979 that the locomotive was seen in specially cleaned condition for the occasion.

M.J.Collins

Nameplates from withdrawn 'Warship' locomotives among those on offer at £515 at 'Collectors' Corner in 1979.

. . . . while No.D832 waits in the research department siding at Egginton Junction bearing the message 'Save me'.
                    Antony R. Guppy

APPENDIX
(official names carried by locos on British Railways to 24 March 1980)

PROTOTYPES

  ---   DELTIC
D0260   LION
D0280   FALCON
10800 * HAWK
HS4000 KESTREL
  --- * TAURUS

*Name never carried

CLASS 40
 Diesel-electric

D210/40.010 EMPRESS OF BRITAIN
D211/40.011 MAURETANIA
D212/40.012 AUREOL
D213/40.013 ANDANIA
D214/40.014 ANTONIA
D215/40.015 AQUITANIA
D216/40.016 CAMPANIA
D217/40.017 CARINTHIA
D218/40.018 CARMANIA
D219/40.019 CARONIA
D220/40.020 FRANCONIA
D221/40.021 IVERNIA
D222/40.022 LACONIA
D223/40.023 LANCASTRIA
D224/40.024 LUCANIA
D225/40.025 LUSITANIA
D227/40.027 PARTHIA
D228/40.028 SAMARIA
D229/40.029 SAXONIA
D230/40.030 SCYTHIA
D231/40.031 SYLVANIA
D232/40.032 EMPRESS OF CANADA
D233/40.033 EMPRESS OF ENGLAND
D234/40.034 ACCRA
D235/40.035 APAPA

CLASS 41
 Diesel-hydraulic ('Warship')

D600 ACTIVE
D601 ARK ROYAL
D602 BULLDOG
D603 CONQUEST
D604 COSSACK

CLASS 42
 Diesel-hydraulic ('Warship')

D800 SIR BRIAN ROBERTSON
D801 VANGUARD
D802 FORMIDABLE
D803 ALBION
D804 AVENGER
D805 BENBOW
D806 CAMBRIAN
D807 CARADOC
D808 CENTAUR
D809 CHAMPION
D810 COCKADE
D811 DARING
D812 * THE ROYAL NAVAL RESERVE 1859-1959
D813 DIADEM
D814 DRAGON
D815 DRUID
D816 ECLIPSE
D817 FOXHOUND
D818 GLORY
D819 GOLIATH
D820 GRENVILLE
D821 GREYHOUND
D822 HERCULES
D823 HERMES
D824 HIGHFLYER
D825 INTREPID
D826 JUPITER

D827   KELLY
D828   MAGNIFICENT
D829   MAGPIE
D830   MAJESTIC
D831   MONARCH
D832   ONSLAUGHT

*D812 originally DESPATCH, nameplates
   made but never carried

CLASS 43
  Diesel-hydraulic ('Warship')

D833   PANTHER
D834   PATHFINDER
D835   PEGASUS
D836   POWERFUL
D837   RAMILLIES
D838   RAPID
D839   RELENTLESS
D840   RESISTANCE
D841   ROEBUCK
D842   ROYAL OAK
D843   SHARPSHOOTER
D844   SPARTAN
D845   SPRIGHTLY
D846   STEADFAST
D847   STRONGBOW
D848   SULTAN
D849   SUPERB
D850   SWIFT
D851   TEMERAIRE
D852   TENACIOUS
D853   THRUSTER
D854   TIGER
D855   TRIUMPH
D856   TROJAN
D857   UNDAUNTED
D858   VALOROUS
D859   VANQUISHER
D860   VICTORIOUS
D861   VIGILANT
D862   VIKING
D863   WARRIOR
D864 * ZAMBESI

D865 * ZEALOUS
D866   ZEBRA
D867   ZENITH
D868   ZEPHYR
D869   ZEST
D870   ZULU

*D864 originally ZEALOUS and
  D865 originally ZENITH,
   neither name ever carried

CLASS 44
  Diesel-electric ('Peak')

D1/44.001   SCAFELL PIKE
D2/44.002   HELVELLYN
D3/44.003   SKIDDAW
D4/44.004   GREAT GABLE
D5/44.005   CROSS FELL
D6/44.006   WHERNSIDE
D7/44.007   INGLEBOROUGH
D8/44.008   PENYGHENT
D9/44.009   SNOWDON
D10/44.010 TRYFAN

CLASS 45
  Diesel-electric ('Peak')

D49/45.039   THE MANCHESTER REGIMENT
D50/45.040   KING'S SHROPSHIRE LIGHT INFANTRY
D52/45.123   THE LANCASHIRE FUSILIER
D53/45.041   ROYAL TANK REGIMENT
D54/45.023   THE ROYAL PIONEER CORPS
D55/45.144   ROYAL SIGNALS
D56/45.137   THE BEDFORDSHIRE AND HERTFORDSHIRE
                REGIMENT (T.A.)
D58/45.043   THE KING'S OWN ROYAL BORDER REGIMENT
D59/45.104   THE ROYAL WARWICKSHIRE FUSILIER
D60/45.022   LYTHAM ST. ANNES
D61/45.112   ROYAL ARMY ORDNANCE CORPS
D62/45.143   5TH ROYAL INNISKILLING DRAGOON GUARDS
D63/45.044   ROYAL INNISKILLING FUSILIER

D64/45.045   COLDSTREAM GUARDSMAN
D65/45.111   GRENADIER GUARDSMAN
D67/45.118   THE ROYAL ARTILLERYMAN
D68/45.046   ROYAL FUSILIER
D70/45.048   THE ROYAL MARINES
D71/45.049   THE STAFFORDSHIRE REGIMENT
              (PRINCE OF WALES'S OWN)
D77/45.004   ROYAL IRISH FUSILIER
D84/45.055   ROYAL CORPS OF TRANSPORT
D89/45.006   HONOURABLE ARTILLERY COMPANY
D98/45.059   ROYAL ENGINEER
D99/45.135   3RD CARABINIER
D100/45.060   SHERWOOD FORESTER
D137/45.014   THE CHESHIRE REGIMENT

CLASS 46
 Diesel-electric ('Peak')

D163/46.026   LEICESTERSHIRE AND DERBYSHIRE
              YEOMANRY

   CLASS 47
    Diesel-electric

   D1660/47.076   CITY OF TRURO
   D1661/47.077   NORTH STAR
   D1662/47.484   ISAMBARD KINGDOM BRUNEL
   D1663/47.078   SIR DANIEL GOOCH
A D1664/47.079   GEORGE JACKSON CHURCHWARD
   D1665/47.080   TITAN
   D1666/47.081   ODIN
   D1667/47.082   ATLAS
   D1668/47.083   ORION
   D1669/47.538   PYTHON
   D1670/47.085   MAMMOTH
B D1671   THOR
   D1672/47.086   COLOSSUS
   D1673/47.087   CYCLOPS
   D1674/47.088   SAMSON
   D1675/47.089   AMAZON
   D1676/47.090   VULCAN
B D1677/47.091   THOR
C D1762/47.167   County of Essex

C D1764/47.169   Great Eastern
C D1765/47.170   County of Norfolk
C D1767/47.172   County of Hertfordshire
C D1775/47.180   County of Suffolk
C D1779/47.184   County of Cambridgeshire
C D1616/47.480   Robin Hood
C D1943/47.500   Great Western
C D1952/47.508   Great Britain
C D1953/47.509   Albion
C D1954/47.510   Fair Rosamund
C D1955/47.511   Thames
C D1959/47.513   Severn
C D1717/47.555   The Commonwealth Spirit
C D1932/47.701   Saint Andrew
C D1947/47.702   Saint Cuthbert
C D1960/47.703   Saint Mungo
C D1937/47.704   Dunedin
C D1957/47.705   Lothian
C D1936/47.706   Strathclyde
C D1949/47.707   Holyrood
C D1968/47.708   Waverley
C D1942/47.709   The Lord Provost
C D1939/47.710   Sir Walter Scott
C D1941/47.711* William Wallace
C D1948/47.712* Prince Charles Edward

A since shortened to G.J.CHURCHWARD
B D1671 was scrapped after collision
   damage and the name transferred to
   D1677 in 1966
C names not carried until after
   renumbering as Class 47

* names reported planned, subject to
   confirmation

*CLASS 50
 Diesel-electric

D400/50.050   Fearless
D401/50.001   Dreadnought
D402/50.002   Superb
D403/50.003   Temeraire
D404/50.004   St. Vincent
D405/50.005   Collingwood
D406/50.006   Neptune
D407/50.007   Hercules

D408/50.008	Thunderer	
D409/50.009	Conqueror	
D410/50.010	Monarch	
D411/50.011	Centurion	
D412/50.012	Benbow	
D413/50.013	Agincourt	
D414/50.014	Warspite	
D415/50.015	Valiant	
D416/50.016	Barham	
D417/50.017	Royal Oak	
D418/50.018	Resolution	
D419/50.019	Ramillies	
D420/50.020	Revenge	
D421/50.021	Rodney	
D422/50.022	Anson	
D423/50.023	Howe	
D424/50.024	Vanguard	
D425/50.025	Invincible	
D426/50.026	Indomitable	
D427/50.027	Lion	
D428/50.028	Tiger	
D429/50.029	Renown	
D430/50.030	Repulse	
D431/50.031	Hood	
D432/50.032	Courageous	
D433/50.033	Glorious	
D434/50.034	Furious	
D435/50.035	Ark Royal	
D436/50.036	Victorious	
D437/50.037	Illustrious	
D438/50.038	Formidable	
D439/50.039	Implacable	
D440/50.040	Leviathan	
D441/50.041	Bulwark	
D442/50.042	Triumph	
D443/50.043	Eagle	
D444/50.044	Exeter	
D445/50.045	Achilles	
D446/50.046	Ajax	
D447/50.047	Swiftsure	
D448/50.048	Dauntless	
D449/50.049	Defiance	

*names not carried until
 after renumbering as
 Class 50

CLASS 52
Diesel-hydraulic ('Western')

D1000	WESTERN ENTERPRISE
D1001	WESTERN PATHFINDER
D1002	WESTERN EXPLORER
D1003	WESTERN PIONEER
D1004	WESTERN CRUSADER
D1005	WESTERN VENTURER
D1006	WESTERN STALWART
D1007	WESTERN TALISMAN
D1008	WESTERN HARRIER
D1009	WESTERN INVADER
D1010	WESTERN CAMPAIGNER
D1011	WESTERN THUNDERER
D1012	WESTERN FIREBRAND
D1013	WESTERN RANGER
D1014	WESTERN LEVIATHAN
D1015	WESTERN CHAMPION
D1016	WESTERN GLADIATOR
D1017	WESTERN WARRIOR
D1018	WESTERN BUCCANEER
D1019	WESTERN CHALLENGER
D1020	WESTERN HERO
D1021	WESTERN CAVALIER
D1022	WESTERN SENTINEL
D1023	WESTERN FUSILIER
D1024	WESTERN HUNTSMAN
D1025	WESTERN GUARDSMAN
D1026	WESTERN CENTURION
D1027	WESTERN LANCER
D1028	WESTERN HUSSAR
D1029 *	WESTERN LEGIONNAIRE
D1030	WESTERN MUSKETEER
D1031	WESTERN RIFLEMAN
D1032	WESTERN MARKSMAN
D1033	WESTERN TROOPER
D1034	WESTERN DRAGOON
D1035	WESTERN YEOMAN
D1036	WESTERN EMPEROR
D1037	WESTERN EMPRESS
D1038	WESTERN SOVEREIGN
D1039	WESTERN KING
D1040	WESTERN QUEEN
D1041	WESTERN PRINCE
D1042	WESTERN PRINCESS

D1043	WESTERN DUKE
D1044	WESTERN DUCHESS
D1045	WESTERN VISCOUNT
D1046	WESTERN MARQUIS
D1047	WESTERN LORD
D1048	WESTERN LADY
D1049	WESTERN MONARCH
D1050	WESTERN RULER
D1051	WESTERN AMBASSADOR
D1052	WESTERN VICEROY
D1053	WESTERN PATRIARCH
D1054	WESTERN GOVERNOR
D1055	WESTERN ADVOCATE
D1056	WESTERN SULTAN
D1057	WESTERN CHIEFTAIN
D1058	WESTERN NOBLEMAN
D1059	WESTERN EMPIRE
D1060	WESTERN DOMINION
D1061	WESTERN ENVOY
D1062	WESTERN COURIER
D1063	WESTERN MONITOR
D1064	WESTERN REGENT
D1065	WESTERN CONSORT
D1066	WESTERN PREFECT
D1067	WESTERN DRUID
D1068	WESTERN RELIANCE
D1069	WESTERN VANGUARD
D1070	WESTERN GAUNTLET
D1071	WESTERN RENOWN
D1072	WESTERN GLORY
D1073	WESTERN BULWARK

*originally WESTERN
•LEGIONAIRE, but nameplates
 were extended

CLASS 55
Diesel-electric ('Deltic')

D9000/55.022	ROYAL SCOTS GREY
D9001/55.001	ST. PADDY
D9002/55.002	THE KING'S OWN YORKSHIRE LIGHT INFANTRY
D9003/55.003	MELD
D9004/55.004	QUEEN'S OWN HIGHLANDER
D9005/55.005	THE PRINCE OF WALES'S OWN REGIMENT OF YORKSHIRE
D9006/55.006	THE FIFE AND FORFAR YEOMANRY
D9007/55.007	PINZA
D9008/55.008	THE GREEN HOWARDS
D9009/55.009	ALYCIDON
D9010/55.010	THE KING'S OWN SCOTTISH BORDERER
D9011/55.011	THE ROYAL NORTHUMBERLAND FUSILIERS
D9012/55.012	CREPELLO
D9013/55.013	THE BLACK WATCH
D9014/55.014	THE DUKE OF WELLINGTON'S REGIMENT
D9015/55.015	TULYAR
D9016/55.016	GORDON HIGHLANDER
D9017/55.017	THE DURHAM LIGHT INFANTRY
D9018/55.018	BALLYMOSS
D9019/55.019	ROYAL HIGHLAND FUSILIER
D9020/55.020	NIMBUS
D9021/55.021	ARGYLL AND SUTHERLAND HIGHLANDER

CLASS 76
Electric

26000	TOMMY
26046/76.046	ARCHIMEDES
26047/76.047	DIOMEDES
26048/76.039	HECTOR
26049/76.049	JASON
26050/76.038	STENTOR
26051/76.051	MENTOR
26052/76.052	NESTOR
26053/76.053	PERSEUS
26054/76.054	PLUTO
26055/76.055	PROMETHEUS
26056/76.056	TRITON
26057/76.057	ULYSSES

CLASS 77
Electric

27000	ELECTRA
27001	ARIADNE
27002	AURORA
27003	DIANA
27004	JUNO
27005	MINERVA
27006	PANDORA

*CLASS 86
  Electric

E3191/86.101 Sir William A Stanier F R S
E3173/86.204 City of Carlisle
E3129/86.205 City of Lancaster
E3184/86.206 City of Stoke-on-Trent
E3141/86.208 City of Chester
E3125/86.209 City of Coventry
E3190/86.210 City of Edinburgh
E3151/86.212 Preston Guild
E3193/86.213 Lancashire Witch
E3166/86.216 Meteor
E3175/86.218 Planet
E3196/86.219 Phoenix
E3156/86.220 Goliath
E3132/86.221 Vesta
E3131/86.222 Fury
E3158/86.223 Hector
E3134/86.224 Caledonian
E3162/86.226 Mail
E3167/86.228 Vulcan Heritage
E3113/86.232 Harold Macmillan
E3194/86.235 Novelty
E3127/86.240 Bishop Eric Treacy
E3121/86.241 Glenfiddich
E3137/86.259 Peter Pan

*names not carried until after
   renumbering as Class 86
Note: further namings are planned
        for Class 86 during 1980

CLASS 87
  Electric

87.001 * Royal Scot
87.002   Royal Sovereign
87.003   Patriot
87.004   Britannia
87.005   City of London
87.006   City of Glasgow
87.007   City of Manchester
87.008   City of Liverpool
87.009   City of Birmingham
87.010   King Arthur
87.011   The Black Prince
87.012   Coeur-de-Lion
87.013   John O'Gaunt
87.014   Knight of the Thistle
87.015   Howard of Effingham
87.016   Sir Francis Drake
87.017   Iron Duke
87.018   Lord Nelson
87.019   Sir Winston Churchill
87.020   North Briton
87.021   Robert the Bruce
87.022   Cock o' the North
87.023   Highland Chieftain
87.024   Lord of the Isles
87.025   Borderer
87.026   Redgauntlet
87.027   Wolf of Badenoch
87.028   Lord President
87.029   Earl Marischal
87.030   Black Douglas
87.031   Hal o' the Wynd
87.032   Kenilworth
87.033   Thane of Fife
87.034   William Shakespeare
87.035   Robert Burns
87.101 * STEPHENSON

*the name STEPHENSON was first
  carried by 87.001 using the
  same nameplates

The process continues, with 11 April 1980 seeing the first naming of a Southern Region diesel. No.33.008 is the locomotive being ceremonially christened by the Mayor of Eastleigh at the station whose name it now carries. A similar ceremony was carried out by the Mayor of Ashford upon 33.052 on 15 May the same year. Scheduled for later in 1980 were namings of the locomotives involved with the funeral train of Earl Mountbatten of Burma, diesels 33.027 and 33.056 to be named 'Earl Mountbatten of Burma' and 'The Burma Star' respectively while the first electro-diesel locomotive to receive a name will be 73.142 'Broadlands' after the Mountbatten estate.

Brian Morrison